UKRAINIAN ENGLISH First W

100 First words Color Picture Book with English Translations and English pronunciation

A perfect **UKRAINIAN English Bilingual First words book!**

- ➤ 28 Color pages, with 100 Words collected and grouped across familiar everyday themes like **family, animals, fruits, vegetables, numbers, hospital, home, body parts** and so on
- ➤ Classic first words are presented in English and UKRAINIAN with bright illustrations/photographic color pictures and pronunciations to help with language comprehension
- ➤ **100 eye-catching** illustrations/ photographs of **familiar things,** each with **big labels color printed underneath in both languages** for easy understanding and comprehension
- ➤ A great aid for building vocabulary and recognizing words in both languages for all little learners.
- ➤ Learn UKRAINIAN and English language with this bilingual 100 first words book, complete with cheerful COLOR illustrations and its pronunciation
- ➤ An ideal tool to teach new words in both English and UKRAINIAN
- ➤ Fun, educational foreign language introduction for preschoolers and kindergarteners
- ➤ Premium color cover design
- ➤ Printed on **high quality** perfectly sized pages at 8.5x11 inches **premium color pages**

UKRAINIAN Alphabets
УКРАЇНСЬКІ АБЕТКИ

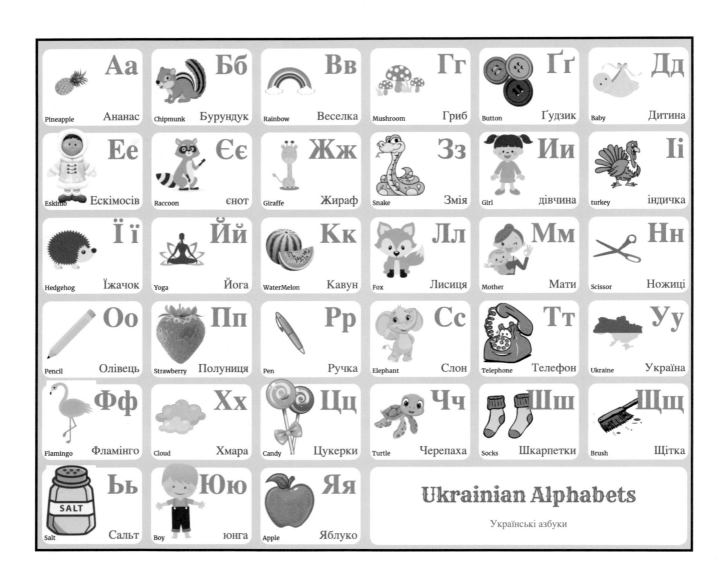

Аа Pineapple — Ананас	**Бб** Chipmunk — Бурундук	**Вв** Rainbow — Веселка
Гг Mushroom — Гриб	**Ґґ** Button — Ґудзик	**Дд** Baby — Дитина
Ее Eskimo — Ескімосів	**Єє** Raccoon — ЄНОТ	**Жж** Giraffe — Жираф
Зз Snake — Змія	**Ии** Girl — дівчина	**Іі** turkey — індичка
Її Hedgehog — Їжачок	**Йй** Yoga — Йога	**Кк** WaterMelon — Кавун
Лл Fox — Лисиця	**Мм** Mother — Мати	**Нн** Scissor — Ножиці
Оо Pencil — Олівець	**Пп** Strawberry — Полуниця	**Рр** Pen — Ручка
Сс Elephant — Слон	**Тт** Telephone — Телефон	**Уу** Ukraine — Україна
Фф Flamingo — Фламінго	**Хх** Cloud — Хмара	**Цц** Candy — Цукерки
Чч Turtle — Черепаха	**Шш** Socks — Шкарпетки	**Щщ** Brush — Щітка
Ьь Salt — Сальт	**Юю** Boy — юнга	**Яя** Apple — Яблуко

Ukrainian Alphabets

Українські азбуки

We hope you love the book!

If so, would you care to leave us a quick review? It would mean a lot to us! Don't forget to checkout the UKRAINIAN Letter Tracing and UKRAINIAN alphabets charts from the author

Fruit

Фрукти

[Frukty]

Apple

яблуко

[yabluko]

Grapes

Виноград

[Vynohrad]

Watermelon

Кавун

[Kavun]

Mango

Манго

[manho]

Banana

Банан

[banan]

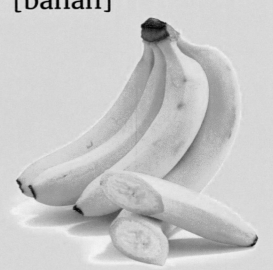

Carrot

Морква

[Morkva]

Vegetables

Овочі

[Ovochi]

Onions
Цибуля
[Tsybulya]

Lemon
Лимонний
[Lymonnyy]

Garlic
Часник
[chasnyk]

Tomato
Томатний
[Tomatnyy]

Mushroom

Гриб

[Hryb]

Pumpkin

Гарбуз

[Harbuz]

Cucumber

Огірок

[ohirok]

Flower

Квітка

[Kvitka]

Bodyparts
Частини тіла
[Chastyna tila]

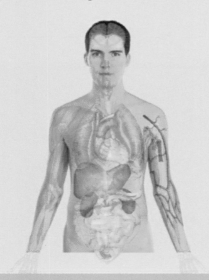

Eye
Око
[Oko]

Ears
Вуха
[Vukha]

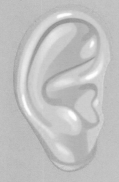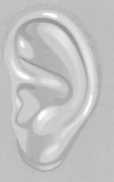

Heart
Серце
[Sertse]

Nose

Hic
[Nis]

Leg

Нога
[Noha]

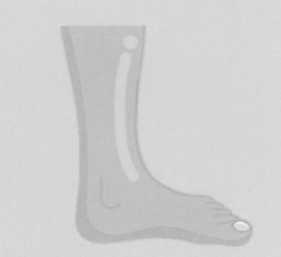

Mustache

Вуса
[Vusa]

Hair

Волосся
[Volossya]

Animals

Тварин
[Tvaryna]

Cat

кіт
[kit]

Dog

Собака
[Sobaka]

Fish

Риба
[ryba]

Lion

Лев

[Lev]

Rabbit

Кролик

[Krolyk]

Snake

Змія

[Zmiya]

Tiger

Тигр

[tyhr]

Horse

Кінь

[Kin']

Alligator

Алігатор

[Alihator]

Donkey

Осел

[osel]

Camel

Верблюд

[Verblyud]

Elephant

Слон

[Slon]

Fox

Лисиця

[lysytsya]

Ant

Мурашка

[Murashka]

Frog

Жаба

[zhaba]

Mosquito

комар

[komar]

Bird

Птах

[Ptakh]

Hen

Курка

[Kurka]

Cow

Корова

[korova]

Goat

Коза
[Koza]

Monkey

Мавпа
[Mavpa]

Bear

Ведмідь
[Vedmid']

Crow

Ворона
[Vorona]

Family

Сім'я

[Sim'ya]

Father

Батько

[Bat'ko]

Mother

Мама

[maty]

Girl

Дівчина

[divchyna]

Boy

Хлопчик

[Khlopchyk]

Daughter

Дочка

[dochka]

Brother

Брат

[brat]

Sister

Сестра

[sestra]

Numbers

Числа
[Chysla]

12345
67890

Zero

Нульовий
[Nul'ovyy]

One

Один
[odyn]

Two

Два
[dva]

Three

Три
[Try]

Four

Чотири
[Chotyry]

Five

П'ять
[p'yat′]

Six

Шість
[shist′]

Seven

Сім

[Sim]

Eight

Вісім

[visim]

Nine

Дев'ять

[dev'yat']

Ten

Десять

[desyat']

Twenty

Двадцять

[Dvadtsyat']

Fifty

П'ятдесят

[P'yatdesyat]

Hundred

СОТНЯ

[sotnya]

Thousand

тисячі

[tysyachi]

Umbrella
Парасолька
[Parasol'ka]

Hat
Капелюх
[Kapelyukh]

Airplane
Літак
[Litak]

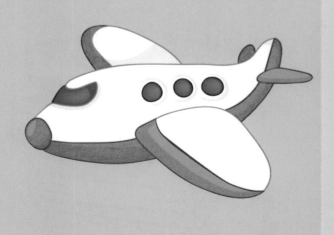

Necklace
Намисто
[Namysto]

Pocket
Кишеньковий
[Kyshen'kovyy]

Glasses
Окуляри
[Okulyary]

Scissors
Ножиці
[Nozhytsi]

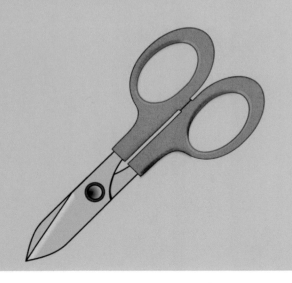

Book
Книга
[Knyha]

Needle

Голка
[holka]

Mirror

Дзеркало
[Dzerkalo]

Water

Вода
[Voda]

Knife

ніж
[nizh]

Ball

М'яч

[M'yach]

Tree

Дерево

[Derevo]

Leaf

Лист

[Lyst]

Questions

Питання

[Pytannya]

Gold
Золото
[Zoloto]

House
Будинок
[Budynok]

ThankYou
Дякую
[Dyakuyu]

Fire
Вогонь
[Vohon']

Plate

Тарілка
[Tarilka]

Sleep

Сон
[Son]

Milk

Молоко
[Moloko]

Spoon

Ложка
[lozhka]

Woman
Жінка
[zhinka]

Man
Людина
[Lyudyna]

Grandmother
Бабуся
[babusya]

Baby
Дитина
[Dytyna]

Other books in the series

Made in United States
Troutdale, OR
01/18/2024